FABULOUS CARS

FABULOUS CARS
OF THE 1920s AND 1930s

RICHARD L. KNUDSON

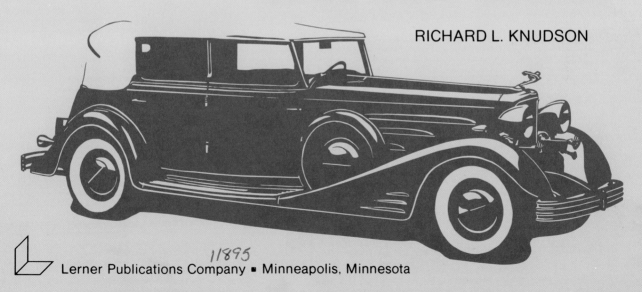

11895

Lerner Publications Company ▪ Minneapolis, Minnesota

ACKNOWLEDGMENTS: All of the photographs in this book have been
provided by Peter Forster for Roth Handle Kunst- und Musikverlag,
Lahr, West Germany, from Harrah's Automobile Collection, Reno,
Nevada, except for the following: p. 6, Ford Motor Company; p. 14,
Indianapolis Motor Speedway Corporation; p. 28, Culver Pictures, Inc.

LIBRARY OF CONGRESS CATALOGING IN PUBLICATION DATA

Knudson, Richard L.
  Fabulous cars of the 1920s and 1930s.

  (Superwheels and thrill sports)
  SUMMARY: Presents a description and history of some of the luxury cars, such as the
Pierce-Arrow Silver Arrow, the Cadillac V-16,
and the Rolls-Royce Phantom III, now part of
the famous Harrah Automobile Collection in
Reno, Nevada.

  1. Automobiles—Juvenile literature. [1. Auto-
mobiles] I. Title. II. Series.

TL147.K58   629.2'222'09042   81-343
ISBN 0-8225-0504-5   AACR1

This edition first published © 1981 by Lerner Publications Company

Text copyright © 1981 by Lerner Publications Company.
Photographs *(except as noted above)* copyright © 1980 by Roth
Handle Kunst- and Musikverlag.
All rights reserved. International copyright secured.

Manufactured in the United States of America

International Standard Book Number: 0-8225-0504-5
Library of Congress Catalog Card Number: 81-343

1 2 3 4 5 6 7 8 9 10 90 89 88 87 86 85 84 83 82 81

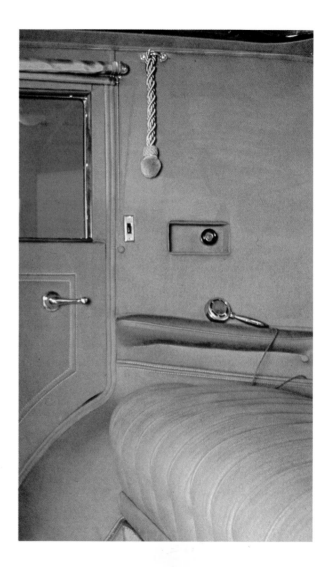

CONTENTS

An early assembly line at a Ford plant. Henry Ford pioneered the methods of mass production that made automobiles inexpensive enough to be owned by ordinary people. But many manufacturers continued to produce luxury models that only the wealthy could afford.

INTRODUCTION

When automobiles first appeared in the United States during the 1890s, they were considered to be playthings for the rich. It wasn't until 1908, when Henry Ford came along with a car inexpensive enough to be owned by ordinary working people, that the automobile became really important as a means of transportation.

Since the automobile started out as a toy for wealthy people, it is not surprising that manufacturers continued to produce luxury models. During the 1920s, there were many customers who wanted to own expensive, high-quality motorcars. Some of these people had made their fortunes during World War I, at a time when industry was booming. Such people were new to the idea of having money, and they wanted to be sure that others knew about their wealth. Owning a fancy automobile such as a Bugatti, a Duesenberg, or a Pierce-Arrow was a very good way to spread the news.

These cars and the others pictured in this book are rolling legends. They are outstanding examples of the best and most expensive automobiles made by American and European manufacturers during the 1920s and 1930s. All of these fabulous cars are found in the world's finest automotive museum, the Harrah Automobile Collection in Reno, Nevada. Well known for its size and its completeness, the Harrah Collection includes more than 1,000 cars representing the history of the automobile from the earliest days to the present. The cars in the collection have been restored to their original

The Duesenberg SJ Speedster was one of the fabulous cars produced in the 1930s.

condition, and all are in perfect running order.

Luxury cars like these from the Harrah Collection are an important part of the history of the automobile. Beautiful, functional, and unusual, they are impressive examples of automotive art. Of course, in our modern energy-conscious world, such cars are no longer practical. Today there are not many people who want to own a big, expensive gas-guzzler no matter how much money they have. We will never see cars such as these manufactured again, but we can enjoy their timeless beauty and appreciate them as reminders of a fascinating era of history.

BUGATTI ROYALE

Ettore Bugatti was one of the most outstanding automobile engineers who ever lived. His career lasted 50 years, and during that time, he designed and built some 9,500 cars, all of which bore his name. Today the approximately 1,900 Bugattis that survive are considered masterpieces of automobile engineering.

Born in Italy in 1881, Ettore Bugatti built his first motorcar at the age of 17. Soon he had established a thriving career as a designer for various Italian, German, and French car manufacturers. Then in 1909, Bugatti moved to France, where he set up his own factory and began to turn out his own unique cars. At first, Bugatti concentrated his efforts on building fast, lightweight race cars. During the 1920s, Bugatti cars won every important automobile race in Europe. With this illustrious record to his credit, why then did Monsieur Bugatti decide to build the Royale —the largest, most luxurious passenger car ever made?

The story goes that one evening at a dinner party, Bugatti was seated next to an English woman who remarked that while Bugatti race cars and sports cars were very fine, only Rolls-Royce could make a really elegant town car. History does not say how the hot-tempered Bugatti reacted to the woman's remarks, but we can be sure that he took them as a challenge.

In 1927, Bugatti revealed to the world his answer to that challenge—the fabulous Bugatti Type 41. Called La Royale or the Golden Bug, it was immediately recognized as the biggest, most elegant, and most expensive motorcar in existence.

Big? The Royale's wheelbase was 14 feet, 2 inches long (a Honda Civic's wheelbase is 6 feet, 6 inches), and its sleek hood measured 7 feet from windshield to radiator cap. Under

Bugatti Royale
Year: *1931*
Engine: *Straight 8, 300 h.p.*

Top Speed: *125 mph*
Original Price: *$42,000*

the hood was an enormous 784-cubic-inch, straight-eight engine that moved the heavy car very efficiently. With the engine turning at only 1,000 revolutions per minute in high gear, the Royale could do 72 miles per hour (mph). The car could cruise at 125 mph without straining the engine one bit.

The Royale's impressive size and power were matched by the elegance of its interior, which included such features as solid ivory fittings on the dashboard. Perhaps most impressive of all was the car's price: $20,000 for the chassis—the frame, engine, and other working parts—plus at least another $10,000 for the body. (Like many other fine cars of this period, the Royale was manufactured and sold as two separate units.)

The Bugatti factory built only six Royales, the first completed in 1927 and the last in 1931. These were the years of the Great Depression, and not many people could afford an automobile that cost over $30,000.

Ettore Bugatti had apparently hoped that his luxurious cars would be purchased by the kings and queens of Europe, but he was disappointed. Not one of the six Royales was sold to a customer with royal blood, although the car shown here was supposed to have been made for King Carol of Rumania.

This Royale is one of two in the Harrah Automobile Collection. (Two other Royales are also in American automobile collections.) Built in 1931, it originally had a two-seater roadster body designed by Ettore Bugatti's son, Jean. The roadster body was later replaced by the handsome *coupé de ville*, or town car, body seen here, which was built by Henri Binder, a well-known French manufacturer of car bodies. Like all of the Royales, this car has as its radiator mascot a proud, trumpeting elephant. What better symbol could there be for the biggest and best automobile that ever cruised down a highway?

MILLER RACE CAR

Most of the cars shown in this book are passenger cars, designed to transport people from place to place in luxury and style. The 1929 Miller pictured here is a race car, and it was designed for just one purpose: to speed around an oval race track in the shortest possible time. Of all the oval tracks in the United States, the one at Indianapolis is the most famous, and the Miller was one of the most successful cars ever to race at Indy.

Opened in 1909, Indy quickly earned a reputation as the best track in the United States. The 500-mile race that has been held there almost every May since 1911 is known the world over as the automobile race with the richest purse and as one of the hardest to win. The first car to take the checkered flag at Indy was a Marmon Wasp, driven by Ray Harroun. In the 1920s, the cars to beat in the Indianapolis 500 were sure to be Millers.

Harry Miller was an automotive genius who dominated American racing for many years. His front-wheel-drive (fwd) cars, like the one in the Harrah collection, were well suited to American oval-track racing because of their superior cornering. Miller's first fwd racer was built in 1924, and two years later, 9 out of the first 10 finishers at Indy were driving Miller cars. In the 1929 race, 27 of the 33 cars on the Indy track had Miller engines, and 7 Millers were among the first 10 cars to cross the finish line.

Harry Miller's cars took 12 checkered flags at Indianapolis before Miller went bankrupt in the early 1930s. His company was taken over by Fred Offenhauser, who had worked with Miller in the 1920s. Offenhauser continued to build race cars and to win consistently in the 500, just as his predecessor had done.

Miller Race Car
Year: *1929*
Engine: *Supercharged Straight 8, 285 h.p.*

Top Speed: *145 mph*
Original Price: *$15,000*

The starting lineup of the 1929 Indianapolis 500-Mile Race included 27 cars with Miller engines. Seven of the Millers were among the first 10 cars to cross the finish line.

The list of Miller wins in American racing is impressive, but the car's influence extended far beyond the oval tracks of the racing world. Harry Miller's use of front wheel drive in his 1924 car was an automotive milestone. The 1929 Cord, the first American fwd passenger to be produced, was modeled after the Miller racer. During 1929, a team of Millers competed in European races to give publicity to the new Cord, and not long after that, the European companies of DKW, Adler and Citroën introduced fwd passenger cars, some of which remained in production for many years.

Back in the United States, Cord went out of business in 1937, but front wheel drive was not dead. In the late 1960s, both Oldsmobile and Cadillac made fwd models, and by 1980, all the U.S. big three—General Motors, Ford, and Chrysler—had front-wheel-drive cars in production.

The technical innovations of the Miller racer even influenced the work of the great European designer Ettore Bugatti, who openly copied the Miller engine in his Type 50, produced in 1932. In his earlier cars, Bugatti had used only one overhead camshaft; the Miller showed him how to use two.

The 1929 Miller in the Harrah collection has been magnificently restored to its original condition. Today visitors to the Harrah museum can take a good look at this 50-year-old engineering masterpiece whose influence on automotive design is still being felt.

Duesenberg Model J Dual-Cowl Phaeton
Year: *1929*　　　　　Top Speed: *115 mph*
Engine: *Straight 8, 265 h.p.*　　Original Price: *$14,000*

DUESENBERG MODELS J AND SJ

Have you ever heard someone say, "It's a doozy!" when they were describing an item that was really special or of extra high quality? This expression is not used much today, but in the 1930s, it was quite common. It originated in connection with the fabulous Duesenberg, the finest automobile ever produced in the United States. Something that was considered as good as a Duesenberg was very good indeed.

Among the Duesenbergs in the Harrah collection are two rare and valuable cars, a 1929 Model J Dual-Cowl Phaeton and a 1933 SJ Speedster. These two models were among the high-performance, luxury cars produced in the late 1920s and early 1930s by the Duesenberg brothers, Frederick and August. Before that time, the Duesenbergs were famous for their powerful race cars. Most of the great drivers of the 1920s, among them Barney Oldfield, Eddie Rickenbacker, Peter de Paolo, and Jimmy Murphy, drove Duesenbergs in competition. Important wins were recorded in the Indianapolis 500 and in the French Grand Prix. Cars with Duesenberg engines also held several speed records, including the 1920 world's land speed record.

This experience in racing not only gave the Duesenberg company good publicity but also helped its engineers test and develop new ideas. One idea that came out of all this competition was the use of four-wheel hydraulic brakes, a Duesenberg original. Despite the Duesenbergs' success in racing, however, their company did not do well. Fred Duesenberg, the leader of the two brothers, was an automotive genius, but he was not very clever in financial matters.

In 1926 the Duesenberg enterprise was taken over by a company that already produced one fine American car, the Auburn. E. L. Cord, the man behind the company, liked Fred Duesenberg's ideas and gave him the chance to build the kind of car he had always dreamed of. The result was the Model J Duesenberg, which first appeared in 1929. The Model J was a doozy of a car, with a 265-horsepower (h.p.) engine and a top speed of 115 mph. The chassis was a work of art, made out of the highest quality steel and polished to a bright finish. A customer paid $8,500 for a Model J chassis and at least $5,000 more for a custom body good enough to go over it.

The body of the Model J Dual-Cowl Phaeton in the Harrah collection was made by a famous coachbuilder of the period named Murphy. This body style is rather unusual. Many cars of the 1920s and 1930s were built as phaetons (FAY-uh-tuns), with folding tops and seats for four passengers, but not many had a second cowl separating the front and back seats. This dual cowl came complete with a windshield and a duplicate set of dashboard instruments so that passengers in the rear seat could keep an eye on the car's speed and performance.

Whatever its body style, the Model J Duesenberg was recognized all over the world as a fine automobile. In the 1930s, many famous and wealthy people owned Model Js — European kings and nobles, American politicians, movie stars, band leaders, and gangsters. Magazine advertisements for the Duesenberg pictured expensively dressed people in luxurious surroundings and included only one line of copy: "He (or she) drives a Duesenberg." Nothing more had to be said.

People who wanted a faster, sportier Duesenberg than the Model J could choose the SJ Speedster, which was introduced in 1933. Equipped with a supercharged engine, the SJ had a maximum speed of 130 mph. It took only 17 seconds to reach 100 mph, and it could do 104 mph in second gear. In 1933,

Duesenberg SJ Speedster
Year: *1933*
Engine: *Supercharged Straight 8, 320 h.p.*

Top Speed: *130 mph*
Original Price: *$17,500*

this was a startling performance for an automobile; even today, few cars can do as well. The SJ was the realization of Fred Duesenberg's dream — to create a car equal to the Rolls-Royce in quality but much faster.

With its streamlined fenders and graceful, pointed boat tail, the SJ Speedster looked fast even when it was standing still. Another conspicuous feature of the car's body was the external exhaust system, with its bright chrome pipes coming out from the side of the hood. Today many people think that this external exhaust has something to do with the SJ's supercharger. Actually there is no connection. A supercharger is a small device attached to the engine that increases the amount of air in the combustion chambers. The kind of external exhaust used on the SJ was also used on other Duesenberg models as well as on various Auburns and Cords produced by the same company.

Like the Model J, the SJ was popular with the wealthy and famous. Two of the great Hollywood stars of the 1930s, Clark Gable and Gary Cooper, owned specially designed versions of the SJ. Such people used the Speedster for personal transportation and did the driving themselves. This was not the kind of car to be driven by a chauffeur.

In 1933, the SJ Speedster cost $17,500. In today's market, a fully restored example of either the Speedster or the Dual-Cowl Phaeton would probably be worth around $250,000! The Duesenberg brothers produced a total of only 650 cars, and today about one-third of them are in the hands of collectors. Many Duesenbergs were no doubt wrecked or scrapped years ago, but there must be others still in existence. Just think —in an old barn somewhere, a Doozy may be waiting to be discovered and restored to its original beauty.

DU PONT MODEL G ROYAL TOWN CAR

Today the name Du Pont makes most people think of paints and chemicals, but at one time it was also associated with cars. Between 1919 and 1932, the Du Pont Company built 547 fine automobiles that rivaled the luxury products of the European manufacturers. Over one-third of Du Pont's entire production was the Model G, one of which is pictured here. This particular car, built in 1930, was known as the Royal Town Car. Its coupé de ville body was constructed by Merrimac of Merrimac, Massachusetts, one of the most popular of the coachbuilders that made bodies for the Du Pont customers.

The coupé de ville style was a favorite of wealthy people, and many luxury cars of the period used it. In a coupé de ville, the chauffeur sat out in the open, just like the driver of an old-fashioned horsedrawn coach. A glass partition separated the chauffeur from the car's passengers, who enjoyed the privacy of the enclosed back seat with its small window area. Many of the people who owned Du Pont Royal Town cars lived in the country and had to travel into the city each day to conduct business. Making the trip by commuter train would have been too inconvenient and too ordinary, but in a Royal Town Car, a wealthy businessman could travel in real style. The car's eight-cylinder, 140-horsepower engine insured that the trip would be speedy as well as comfortable.

In the early 1930s, the United States, along with the rest of the world, was in the middle of a great economic depression. During this period, many companies, especially automobile manufacturers, went out of business. Du Pont stopped making cars in 1932, but of course the huge company did not fail. The automobile factory was only a small part of the Du Pont empire, and it had probably never made much money anyway since it had

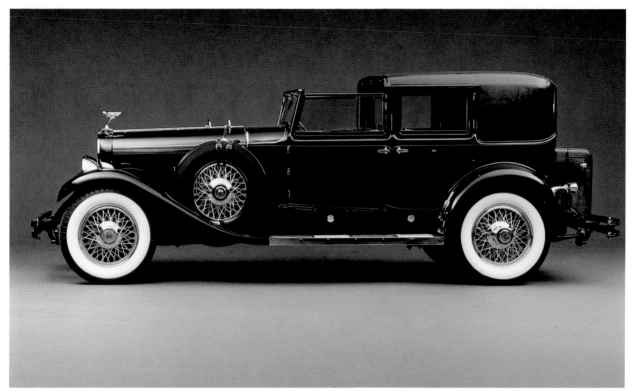

Du Pont Model G Royal Town Car
Year: *1930*　　　　Top Speed: *80 mph*
Engine: *Straight 8, 140 h.p.*　　Original Price: *$5,750*

produced such a small number of cars over the years. With so few customers for expensive automobiles during the depression, Du Pont simply decided to get out of the car business and concentrate on its other varied interests.

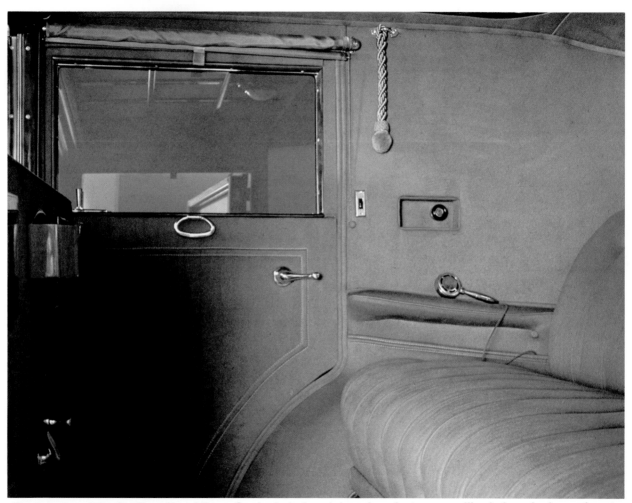

The interior of the Du Pont Royal Town Car included such luxurious features as silk window shades and seats upholstered in pink velvet.

Packard Phaeton
Year: *1929*
Engine: *Straight 8, 106 h.p.*
Top Speed: *75 mph*
Original Price: *$4,935*

PACKARD PHAETON AND SPORT PHAETON

What the legendary Rolls-Royce was to England in the 1920s and 1930s, Packard was to the United States. This American car had a reputation for quality, excellence, and luxury that was established early and maintained for a long time. As a result, rich and important people all over the world bought Packards. Several United States presidents, among them Franklin D. Roosevelt, used an armored version of the Packard for their official transportation.

The Packard was born around the turn of the century, brought into existence by one man's dissatisfaction with another automobile. In 1898 James Ward Packard, an engineer in Warren, Ohio, bought a brand new Winton motorcar in nearby Cleveland. On the drive home he had several breakdowns, but when he complained to the manufacturer of the car, Alexander Winton, he got no results. In fact, Winton told Packard that if he didn't like the car, he should go out and build a better one himself. Packard accepted the challenge, and on November 6, 1899, the first Packard automobile rolled down the streets of Warren. It *was* a better product, and the newly formed company quickly established itself as a manufacturer of quality automobiles.

In 1903 Packard produced one of the first 4-cyclinder cars, but it was a 12-cylinder engine that made the company well known. Introduced in 1915 at a time when other manufacturers of luxury cars were producing 4s, 6s, and 8s, the Packard V-12—also known as the Twin Six—was very successful. In 1923, however, the V-12 was replaced by a straight-8, and it was this engine that became the standard power source for most future Packards.

From 1899 until it ceased production in 1958, the Packard Company made 1,610,890 motorcars. This large number puts Packard in a different category from that of most other manufacturers of luxury cars, whose production was much smaller. During its day, Packard had the majority of the world's luxury car market in its pocket. Although the company did produce a line of cheaper cars in the 1930s and 1940s, its main efforts were always concentrated on producing fine automobiles for those people who could afford to buy the best.

The Harrah Collection includes around 50 Packards. William Harrah, the owner of the collection, is especially interested in American automobiles and eventually wants to have a Packard and a Ford from each year that these two important makes were produced. One of the two Harrah Packards shown here—the Model 645 Phaeton—was built in 1929. This car is a good example of the sort of luxury vehicle that appealed to wealthy people who wanted to be seen. Because it was a Packard, it let people know that the owner was rich. Even if observers didn't know what kind of a car it was, the presence of a uniformed chauffeur would be an important clue. Compared to a town car, the phaeton body didn't provide much privacy, but with the top down, the passengers could enjoy the sun and breeze on a nice day. They could also be seen by as many people as possible while they were touring the countryside.

The 1934 Sport Phaeton also communicated wealth to observers, but the car emphasized pleasure driving as much as luxury. It was one of a series of expensive 12-cylinder cars that Packard began producing in 1932. With a 160-h.p. engine and a top

Packard Sport Phaeton
Year: *1934*
Engine: *V-12, 160 h.p.*
Top Speed: *100 mph*
Original Price: *$7,820*

Movie star Clark Gable was one of the celebrities who drove a racy Packard Sport Phaeton during the 1930s.

speed of 100 mph, this new Twin Six was a performance automobile that was a joy to drive. The beautiful body, built by LeBaron, had a sports car look because of its sweeping fenders and racy tail.

Twin Sixes like the Sport Phaeton were purchased by Clark Gable and other well-to-do celebrities, but there weren't many buyers for such a high-priced car in the 1930s. The model was taken out of production in 1939 after about 6,000 cars had been built.

PIERCE-ARROW SILVER ARROW

During the Great Depression of the 1930s, many of the luxury car manufacturers in the United States were forced out of business. Most were victims of poor sales, but some companies failed because their cars did not keep up with the times. A few manufacturers of luxury automobiles tried to stay alive by lowering their quality. Pierce-Arrow, however, was a company that died with dignity, its last hopes placed on a magnificent car, the Silver Arrow.

Pierce-Arrow got its start in the early 1900s, beginning with steam cars and producing its first gasoline-powered car in 1902. By 1920, the company was known as a manufacturer of quality automobiles worthy to provide transportation for American presidents and people from the highest social class. A Pierce-Arrow advertising slogan from the 1920s claimed that owners would never be embarrassed by having their cars mistaken for some less distinguished make because "everybody recognizes a Pierce-Arrow."

No other American manufacturer put more emphasis on quality and fine workmanship than Pierce-Arrow. Every car the company made was carefully assembled by master craftsmen out of the highest quality materials. This high standard also meant high prices, although usually not quite as high as the $60,000 that a Persian shah paid in 1930 for a Pierce-Arrow with jewel-encrusted doors and gold-plated bumpers and radiator. Everybody recognized a Pierce-Arrow, but only the rich could afford one.

Like all luxury car makers, Pierce-Arrow ran into trouble during the depression. Most customers did not have the money to buy expensive cars. To attract the few who could afford such luxuries, the Pierce-Arrow engineers created a very advanced automobile, the Silver Arrow, which was introduced in 1933.

The stylish radiator grille of the Silver Arrow

The Silver Arrow had an elegant stream-lined body that had been thoroughly tested in a wind tunnel. The car's advanced styling was not only good looking but also practical; the wind-cheating design made it possible for the Silver Arrow to reach speeds around 120 mph—very fast for 1933. The V-12 engine produced 175 h.p. and had such advanced technical features as seven main bearings (to-day most engines have five), an oil cooler, and hydraulic valve lifters. Technical advances appeared in other parts of the car, for instance, in the power brakes, which made the Silver Arrow as good at stopping as it was in speeding along the highway.

The Silver Arrow was a spectacular car, but with a $10,000 price sticker, it was doomed to fail. The public just wasn't interested. Pierce-Arrow produced only 10 Silver Arrows, and over the next few years, the company quietly went out of business. But at least it had died trying—the Silver Arrow was a true rolling legend.

Pierce-Arrow Silver Arrow
Year: *1933* Top Speed: *120 mph*
Engine: *V-12, 175 h.p.* Original Price: *$10,000*

Auburn Speedster
Year: *1933*   Top Speed: *100 mph*
Engine: *V-12, 160 h.p.* Original Price: *$1,495*

AUBURN SPEEDSTER

Someone once said that "imitation is the highest form of flattery." In the classic car world, flattery by imitation takes the form of *replicars*—reproductions of various classic automobiles such as Bugatti, Mercedes, Cord, Porsche, and Jaguar. All of the replicars are expensive, but the most costly is the Auburn Speedster. This particular replicar has a big price tag not only because it is a good reproduction but also because the original was such an outstanding motorcar.

Auburn Speedsters were produced in the late 1920s and early 1930s by a company in Indiana that had been in the automobile business since 1900. In 1924, the management of the Auburn Company had been taken over by a bright young man named E. L. Cord. Two

years later, Cord added Duesenberg to his growing automobile empire, and the result was the fabulous Duesenberg Model J, introduced in 1929. The Auburn branch of the Cord empire brought out the first Speedster model in 1928. It had the pointed boat tail that marked it as a sports car and that became the trademark for all the Speedsters that would follow.

The Speedster pictured here was produced in 1933. In contrast to the earlier V-8 Speedsters, it had a huge V-12 engine and was intended to compete with the powerful V-12 and V-16 automobiles that Cadillac and other companies were bringing out at this time. The V-12 Speedster was powerful and fast; it developed 160 h.p., and its top speed was

The Auburn Speedster was a powerful and elegant car, but it was not a big seller.

100 mph. It was also a beautiful car, with dashing, sporty lines emphasized in this model by the contrasting colors of the paint job.

Despite its beauty and its high performance, the V-12 Auburn Speedster did not sell well. The depression no doubt had something to do with the lack of sales, but most historians think the real problem was that the Speedster was too cheap! Those people who were in the market for a high-performance car did not believe that the Speedster could be any good since it cost less than $2,000.

In 1935, Auburn brought out yet another Speedster, this one with a straight-eight engine boosted by a supercharger designed by Augie Duesenberg. Each 851 delivered to a dealer had a plaque on its dashboard stating that the car had been driven at 100.2 mph or 100.5 mph or whatever speed that particular car had reached. None was under 100 mph.

The 851 Speedster and its successor, the 852, were the last cars that Auburn produced. By 1938, the Cord empire was out of business, and the unique cars it had created were on their way to becoming collector's items.

CADILLAC V-16 PHAETON

Among the few American automobile manufacturers that survived the economic disasters of the 1930s was Cadillac, a company that began producing fine cars in 1902 and is still turning them out today. Cadillac remains the outstanding American manufacturer of luxury automobiles because the company has never given up its early aim to build "the most moderately priced, strictly high-grade motorcar in the world."

While its first cars may not have been the most beautiful on the road, Cadillac quickly developed a reputation for engineering advances that gave owners a sense of pride as well as security. Starting out with a single-cylinder engine, the company began producing four-cylinder models in 1905. Then in 1914, Cadillac adopted the very advanced idea of a V-8.

The Cadillacs manufactured during this period were outstanding not only for their engineering but also for the precision with which they were made. This was proved in a dramatic test conducted by England's Royal Automobile Club in 1908. Three new Cadillacs were completely disassembled and their parts mixed together. Then some British mechanics were given the job of rebuilding the three cars out of the pile of jumbled parts. Everything fitted together perfectly, and the reassembled Cadillacs passed a 500-mile driving test with flying colors. This was a remarkable achievement in a period when interchangeable automobile parts were almost unknown.

During the 1920s, Cadillac continued to make advances in engineering. In 1923 the company began using four-wheel brakes. Five

Cadillac V-16 Phaeton
Year: *1938*
Engine: *V-16, 165 h.p.*
Top Speed: *100 mph*
Original Price: *$8,300*

years later, Cadillac became the first manufacturer in the world to offer synchro-mesh transmission, which made it possible to change gears without double-clutching—that is, without shifting into neutral and releasing the clutch before shifting into the desired gear. Then the company decided to offer its customers something really special: a car with a 16-cylinder engine.

The Model 452, introduced in 1930, was the first V-16 production car known to the motoring world. This unusual car, with its smooth and silent 165-h.p. engine, firmly established Cadillac as an important manufacturer of luxury automobiles. The V-16 pictured here is a 1933 model with a phaeton body by Fleetwood, the regular Cadillac bodymaker. It has a 148-inch wheelbase, but the beautiful design of the body draws attention to the car's elegance rather than its great size. In fact, without something to compare it to, you might find it hard to believe that the V-16 Phaeton is a massive car with a truly huge engine.

The Cadillac V-16 was produced for 10 years, from 1930 to 1940, but the early models are the ones regarded as classic automobiles today. They combine the highest mechanical excellence with a simple yet beautiful body design. With cars such as these in its background, it is no surprise that Cadillac is still a world leader in automble manufacturing.

MERCEDES 500K ROADSTER

Mercedes-Benz motorcars earned their reputation for excellence by winning the most important races in the world. In Europe more than in the United States, success in competition has always been important in selling passenger cars. No other make has done as well in this area as Mercedes.

The Mercedes-Benz Company can trace its history back to the very first automobiles. As early as 1886, a man named Karl Benz was making cars in Mannheim, Germany. At about the same time, also in Germany, Wilhelm Mayback and Gottlieb Daimler were manufacturing automobiles they called Daimlers. In 1900 the Daimler Company produced the first Mercedes, named after the daughter of one of its designers, and by 1903, the big, white cars were winning races all over Europe. One of their most sensational victories came in 1914, when Mercedes took first, second, and third place in the French Grand Prix. Then in 1926, the Daimler and Benz firms merged and began producing the Mercedes-Benz. The company's racing team regularly took the checkered flag in European races during the 1930s and again in the 1950s.

Beginning in the early 1920s, Mercedes cars made great use of superchargers, those useful gadgets that increase the power of a car's engine by forcing more air into its combustion chambers. Most manufacturers in this period used superchargers that were always engaged, but Mercedes developed one that could be used only when the driver wanted it. When the supercharger was engaged at, say, 90 mph, the engine's power was immediately boosted by 10 percent and the car would shoot ahead to 100 mph. Another unusual feature of the Mercedes supercharger was that it blew air through the carburetor rather than sucking it through. This created a screaming sound that became a trade mark of cars bearing the three-pointed star, the famous Mercedes emblem.

Mercedes 500K Roadster
Year: *1936*
Engine: *Supercharged Straight 8, 160 h.p.*

Top Speed: *105 mph*
Original Price: *$10,780*

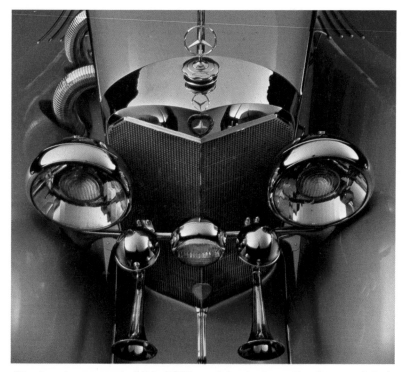

The hood ornament of this 500K roadster features the three-pointed star that is the emblem of Mercedes-Benz.

The model 500K Mercedes, which was produced in the 1930s, featured both the well-known star emblem and the ear-splitting supercharger. The 1936 500K roadster pictured here is an outstanding example of the combined beauty and engineering excellence that was, and is, typical of Mercedes-Benz cars. The lines of the body sweep back from the handsome grille, creating an illusion of grace and speed. Tasteful accents of chrome emphasize the simple lines and curves that make the 500K such an elegant car.

The style of the 500K roadster is obvious; its speed and comfort have to be experienced. The car could easily top 100 mph, and its careful engineering meant that handling, cornering, and braking were without equal.

Any way you look at it, the 500K is a Mercedes—part of a tradition of automotive excellence that the Mercedes-Benz Company has maintained since the early 1900s.

HISPANO-SUIZA TYPE 68

When English-speaking people in the 1930s tried to pronounce the name of this handsome European car, they usually came out with something that sounded like *Banana-squeezer*. The name is really pronounced *ees-PAHN-oh SWEE-zah*, and it means simply "Spanish-Swiss." Hispano-Suiza cars were originally manufactured in Spain and designed by a Swiss-born designer named Marc Birkigt.

In 1899, Birkigt had gone to Barcelona, where he found some Spanish investors willing to help him get started in the automobile business. Five years later, the Hispano-Suiza company was established. The company's first success came when its cars won several important races in 1909. During this period, most small racing cars had either one-cylinder or two-cylinder engines, but the Hispano-Suiza cars were powered by a four-cylinder engine designed by Birkigt.

During World War I, Marc Birkigt and his company took time out from automobile manufacturing to design and build excellent airplane engines that were used in most European fighter planes. One of France's best pilots, Captain Georges Guynemer, flew a SPAD plane with a Hispano-Suiza engine. On the side of the French ace's plane appeared the image of a flying stork, the symbol of the French province of Lorraine. Birkigt admired the gallant Captain Guynemer, who was killed during the war, and he adopted the flying stork as the Hispano-Suiza radiator ornament.

After the war ended in 1918, the flying stork emblem began to appear on some of the world's finest automobiles. One of them was the Hispano-Suiza Type 68, pictured here. Built in 1937, the Type 68 was equipped with a 12-cylinder engine that was well-engineered, powerful, and fast. There was

Hispano-Suiza Type 68
Year: *1937*   Top Speed: *110 mph*
Engine: *V-12, 220 h.p.*   Original Price: *$26,500 (approximate)*

no other passenger car of the late 1930s that could match its performance.

When the Type 68 was introduced at the Paris Auto Show in 1937, an unusual demonstration was staged to prove how well-engineered the engine really was. A prominent journalist, Charles Faroux, drove the car at top speed from Paris to Nice and back, a distance of almost 450 miles (about 720 kilometers). When he arrived in Paris, he went directly to the auto show and drove the Hispano-Suiza onto a large piece of white paper. The crowd watched for a long time, but not one drop of oil or grease fell from the car onto the spotless paper.

The Type 68 was famous not only for the power of its engine but for the elegant lines of its body. The car shown here has the kind of body known as a *berline*, with both front and back seats enclosed but separated by a glass partition. It was constructed by Letourneur and Marchand, one of the famous coachbuilding firms of this period.

Like many other manufacturers, Hispano-Suiza supplied only the chassis of its cars. A customer would take the chassis to a coach-builder who would make a custom body for the car based on certain standard body styles such as the berline, the coupé de ville, and the phaeton. Purchasers of the Hispano-Suiza Type 68 paid $13,260 for the chassis alone and about the same amount for the

Like many automobiles of this period, the Hispano-Suiza Type 68 had both doors hinged at the center post. Today the front doors of most cars are hinged in the front so that they cannot easily be blown open when the cars are moving.

sleek metal body that covered it.

Hispano-Suizas like the Type 68 were great cars, combining speed and comfort with the ultimate in luxury. Today many wealthy and important people fly about the country in private Lear jets, but in the 1930s, such people would have traveled in swift and elegant Hispano-Suizas.

ROLLS-ROYCE PHANTOM III

One of the many legends about the legendary Rolls-Royce is that the hood of each new car is locked shut in the factory. This is supposed to be done for one of two reasons: 1) Only factory mechanics are allowed to work on a Rolls-Royce engine, or 2) The engine is so good that it will never need any work. A good story, but actually none of it is true. The hood isn't locked, and even a Rolls-Royce engine needs some attention after it leaves the factory.

The Rolls-Royce isn't perfect, but it is a very good automobile. The manufacturer's slogan—The Best Car in the World—may not be too far from the truth. Certainly Rolls-Royce has faith in its own product since it guarantees each new car for three years. A Rolls-Royce (never call one a mere Rolls) is made to last; 100,000 miles on the odometer is nothing, and in fact, many Rolls-Royces have to be driven 300,000 miles before they are even broken in.

The company that produces this magnificent car got its start about 75 years ago when two Englishmen named Rolls and Royce formed a partnership. Frederick Henry Royce was an engineer who was fanatic about craftsmanship and quality. In 1903, Royce was producing a reliable two-cylinder automobile, but he was having trouble marketing it. Then he met Charles Stewart Rolls, a wealthy, rather wild young man who enjoyed such things as driving race cars and riding in hot-air balloons. In 1904, the company of Rolls-Royce Limited was formed, and one year later, its first car was on the market.

Rolls-Royce Phantom III
Year: *1938*
Engine: *V-12, 165 h.p.*
Top Speed: *100 mph*
Original Price: *$22,750*

Rolls-Royce established a reputation for its automobiles by racing them in a variety of events, often with Charles Rolls at the wheel. While a Rolls-Royce did not always win a race, it usually impressed people with its quality and ability to finish. In 1907, the company really made an impression when it produced the Silver Ghost, a six-cylinder masterpiece of engineering and construction.

In 1910, Charles Stewart Rolls was killed while piloting an early airplane in a contest. Shortly after his partner's death, Frederick Royce became ill. He retired to Europe and ran the company from a villa on the Riviera until his own death in 1933. At that time, the company directors changed the color of the famous Rolls-Royce double-R trademark from red to black.

The Rolls-Royce shown here is a 1938 Phantom III coupé de ville. As its name indicates, the Phantom III was preceded by two other Phantoms, produced in 1925 and 1919. The earlier models had 6-cylinder engines, but the P-III, which was introduced in 1935, had a 12-cylinder engine, the only Rolls-Royce with such a feature. Its top speed was 100 mph.

The coupé de ville body of this particular Phantom III was built by a French coach-builder named Franay. Compared to the other luxury town cars in this book, the car has a more gently rounded shape in its passenger compartment. The elegance of the P-III's lines suggests the elegance of the interior, with its lush upholstery, fine walnut trim, and varied accessories.

Like other town cars, the Rolls-Royce Phantom III had a glass partition that separated the passenger compartment from the chauffeur's seat.

Two features that the P-III shares with other Rolls-Royce models are the distinctive square grille of the radiator and the Flying Lady radiator mascot. These symbols say "Rolls-Royce" to the world. They have come to represent an automobile with two outstanding characteristics: the silence of its ride and the quality of its materials and workmanship. When a Rolls-Royce drives by, the only sound that can be heard is the hissing of the tires on the pavement. For the passengers inside the car, there is complete silence. Such an amazingly quiet ride can be achieved only by observing the highest standards of quality. Frederick Royce believed that "quality will be remembered long after the price has been forgotten," and the Rolls-Royce company still operates according to that principle.

PHANTOM CORSAIR

Looking something like Darth Vader from outer space, the Phantom Corsair is a stunning example of advanced automotive design. Many of the ideas used in this car are still considered futuristic, yet the Corsair was built in 1938! If the automobile were driven down Main Street in any city today, heads would turn and people would stare. They would find it hard to believe that the design was over 40 years old.

The Phantom Corsair was designed by Rust Heinz, the son of H.J. Heinz (the canned soup millionaire), and it was his ability to see into the future that made the car such a success in concept. The elegant body, built by Bohman and Schwartz, was loaded with new ideas. Notice that there was no door handle or lock; instead there was a

Phantom Corsair
Year: *1938* Top Speed: *115 mph*
Engine: *V-8, 190 h.p.* Original Price: *$25,000*

push button that opened the door electrically. The same button raised a portion of the roof to permit easy entrance into the low-slung car. The only drawback to this magical system was that a dead battery meant the owner stayed outside.

The inside of the Corsair was as luxurious as the outside. Red leather covered all the surfaces, and a great deal of cork and rubber insulated the passengers from sounds as well as making the car very safe. The Corsair's small rear compartment held two passengers, who sat facing the back of the car. The unusually wide front seat accommodated three passengers in addition to the driver: one sat to the driver's left and two to the right.

The chassis used in the Corsair was the same as that in the Cord 810, a front-wheel-drive car that was introduced in 1936. The eight-cylinder engine produced 190 h.p. and moved the two-ton car at over 100 mph.

The prototype of the Phantom Corsair cost $25,000 to build, and production models were scheduled to be made at $12,500. Unfortunately the car never went into production. Its creator, Rust Heinz, was killed in 1939, and the project died with him. The Corsair prototype had its day in the spotlight when it was used in a 1938 movie, *The Young at Heart*, which also featured such glamorous stars as Janet Gaynor and Douglas Fairbanks, Jr. After that, the car disappeared until 1971, when it was discovered and acquired for the Harrah collection. Now this one-of-a-kind car is on display for everyone to see.

In 1938, the Phantom Corsair was called the car of the future. In 2038, the car will probably look as advanced as it did in the days when Douglas Fairbanks, Jr., sat behind the steering wheel.

Superwheels & Thrill Sports

Lerner Publications Company
241 First Avenue North, Minneapolis, Minnesota 55401